Poetry

Against the Falling Evil

The Lover's Familiar

Four Good Things

Each in a Place Apart

The World at Large: New and Selected Poems, 1971–1996

Nonfiction

The Style of the Short Poem

"Ulysses" and Justice

CAPACITY

Capacity · James McMichael

FARRAR, STRAUS AND GIROUX

NEW YORK

FARRAR, STRAUS AND GIROUX
19 Union Square West, New York 10003

Distributed in Canada by Douglas & McIntyre Ltd.
Printed in the United States of America
First edition, 2006

Grateful acknowledgment is made to the following
publications, in which some of these poems originally appeared:
Kenyon Review, The Notre Dame Review, At Length, Chicago Review,
and *American Poetry Review.*

Library of Congress Cataloging-in-Publication Data
McMichael, James, 1939–
    Capacity / James McMichael.— 1st ed.
        p.   cm.
    ISBN-13: 978-0-374-11890-7 (alk. paper)
    ISBN-10: 0-374-11890-6 (alk. paper)
    1. Nature—Poetry. 2. Human ecology—Poetry. 3. Natural resources
—Poetry.   I. Title.

PS3563.A31894C37 2006
811'.54—dc22

                                                        2005051628

Designed by Gretchen Achilles

www.fsgbooks.com

1 3 5 7 9 10 8 6 4 2

They told me last night there were ships in the offing,
And I hurried down to the deep rolling sea,
    But my eye could not see it,
    Wherever might be it,
The bark that is bearing my lover to me.

TRAD.

Someone far from harbor
You may guide across the bar, . . .

CONTENTS

CAPACITY

The frontispiece fixes as
British
a man whose
livelihood is the grass. As he had

before the take and
since,

he plies away in the sun.

"Market Day."
Storefront awnings slope into the square.
Among the occupied,
only the vendors are without hats.
Well-fatted,

sweet and full of pickle are the hooked gibbets of
beef above the pens.
The plate after

"Tractors on Parade" is untitled.
Where the village high street's

walls converge at the far end,
a motor-car has entered and parked.
Pictured empty in another,
the new Great West Road has working

fields to either side. In the one format,

affordable and bound print by print,
grass advances as a factor
never to be run out of by a

people at home.
The farmer is to be seen as having at last put
dearth right.
Nature was on its
own side always. Necessary

against nature sometimes to forbear from making
more mouths to feed.
With the poorest twelfth begetting
half the nation,

the interests of soil and
race were served
by the politics of the straight furrow.

In the countryside
alone it was that one was spared meeting

the less right sort of girl.
Need.
It had become at last what only
others knew,
even if they were in one's midst.

Outside in

Kenya,
Madras,
Shaanxi,

Quixeramobim,
nature had put in place
disastrous shortfalls,
need and epidemic,
nature had played out

Ireland again.
Of those invisible millions who were gone,

nothing was missing.

Nothing was missing
for them. There without need,
they were the revenant in England's garden,
they were the ones whose absence is their sign.

Of the unperceived who keep
safehold where they hide,

vision is a forgetting.
The British were those whom nature let bring home
as graveclothes to the ones it starved

arboreal and floral plantings.
England was green.
There belonged
ill-matched to many their likely

allotments of soil.
Across the range of them from
kitchen-gardens to pleasance,
these were not brandished. They were kept up.
While there were throwback native

cottagers who grew potatoes,

a weekly show on
gardening was aired.
All crystal sets picked up the BBC.

Because those grounds least frequented
were grounds where need was least,

of most
avail was a garden if
no one was there.
The walled reserve was model.
Its expert and only

viewers were staff.

What showed above the fine clean tilth was
surplus.
From its abounding
beds each day,

staff saw to it
for one:
by the garden's having made an
excess of nature,
nature was trumped.

Need had been made less natural.
Replaced was the old
productive ideal that the useful

good was desired.

The desired good was
useful in the new ideal.

Things become useless in the hoarding of them.
Needed for a nation's
surfeit of goods were buyers
primed by their wanting. Desire's

deputy
was the person in love.
An appetite need not slacken if what one

craves is the scarce,
and there is but the one beloved

only.
No hunger
feeds so on itself
as being able
never to have one's fill of someone prized.

They had become friends.

It would not have
occurred to him that she did not
love him. Of

course she did.
Friends love one another.
It began to explain his finding now that
along with love she also

gives him desire. Under something the
sway of which is undue,
in love with her,
he learns that he has had cleared
inside him

a constructed

garden-like place.
He practices his absence

as the stilled reflecting surface of its pool.
With features of her person in his
stead there,
to what is not its

own anymore in wanting

the self is sent
back by the other.
Far enough beyond
reason already is any
one such transport. Improbable

twice over
that with the same conclusive keenness

she should want him.
He looks for cues that
he too had given

her desire.
They are not there.
There is the coming
war to think of as well.
With conscription on its way,

better to be no more than
genial with her for now.
That is why it is her
suitcases he reaches for when he

meets her at the St Pancras train.
Right from the start he is off ahead of her
efficiently down the platform.

Against him from behind,
her fingers have it in them

that she will have to break away

too soon again for her return north.
Out of her greeting hand on his
back he walks.
For no longer than withdrawal

itself takes,
her touch had been there.

Wondering at its light
circumspect grace,
he does not mistake its bidding. What
she wants
he can from this time on want

for her. There can be no

help for them now since what
she wants is him.
Made nearly

bearable by desire is one's not being able to
withstand the desired.
The hurried meetings follow.
Their wanting one another comes to take on
greed as its base.

From the next moment between them
least likely to be surpassed
they carry
away from one another into their days away

more wanting.
It will be weeks.
To be with her

through them instead. If they could be already
beyond the war and

years on,

they might have lives.
Whole patches of days would have to be
discordant, humdrum.
Rote would help them through.

Given ordinary times to

lift her from,
have her lift him,
he would have come to

preside with her over their chances. Around them
everywhere was the petition that

dailiness might hold its gracious own.
Toward it came
sandbags on the corner pavements.
Post office pillar-boxes were rigged with
gas-detecting paint.

The mask itself smelled of rubber. What one saw

first through its eyeshield was one's own
canister snout.
Leaflets from the Lord Privy
Seal's Office were

"Evacuation: Why and How"
and "If the Invader Comes."
So the enemy might

lose themselves in their confusion, the stations'
signposts came down. There were now
barrage balloons overhead
and searchlights.
The Anderson shelter was

corrugated steel.
It needed a garden to be sunk in.

Two million more acres were to come under the plough.
Collected for their great trek
out of the city,
the children walked

"crocodile" to the trains,
a loudspeaker telling them,
"Don't play with the doors and
windows, if you don't mind, thank you."
Villages and towns were to accept a number

equal to their populations.
Each child had a pinned label.

Each was allowed one toy.
They were met at the other end
by strangers who had come to

see who they were.

A lady with a clipboard sought billets for them.
Some of them were in tatters.
The more doleful were often the last picked.
This was to be where they would
live now for a time,

out here in the country.
Files of them traipsed the lanes behind their teachers.
They were shown how to strip
hopbines,

how to make rush baskets out of reeds.
Boys served as beaters for the pheasant-shoots.
Harvest of course meant that

sheaves had to be carted. The sturdier of

both sexes
were put to work in the fields.

No bombs fell into the warm, beautiful autumn.
Most of the children went back home.
When it was time to
leave again for the country,

few of them did.

Above the blackouts,
the Germans were led at first by
moonlight up the Thames estuary.
Then it was by the fires.
Sounding like

stones being thrown at the front wall,
the incendiaries melted steel.

Bombs that screamed their way into the city
thudded down.
A smell of cordite followed.

Looked to be needed each month
were twenty million feet of seasoned
coffin-timber. There were
no more blue waterproof bags.
With the raids coming every night but one,

the dead might have to be dumped in the channel.

It is in bodies given to be seen that
ghosts meet their term.
Their transparency is no less restive.

Escapes that would fail are
patent already

in the pre-war countryside exposed.
Phantom in a picture are gaps that might have been
filled by a child.
One plate is called

"A Quiet Corner."

A trading-wherry is about to tie up.
Full sunlight has
to itself again for the afternoon
the bench
an East End child had jumped from for her

sprint to the canal. She had seen that
ropes needed securing. Having
called to her up the slope,
the bargeman was mindful that at

that same lock last spring
a man had asked to take his picture.

There are pollarded
willows in the picture. In another,
a hedge-crowned wall.

Stills of the countryside are composures.
They apply to keeping
outcome at bay.
Nameable,

all finite things are
present to one another for as
long as they show.
The bedding planes first. Ready
never to be seen as country,

they are exposed sometimes as its side.
On show in their single plots,
slate, shale and

weald clay,

marl,
the Tertiaries,

chalk and upper greensand.
A former seafloor laid down
shell by shell,

limestone dislikes interruption.
As stuffs from its lighter understories wear away,
streams take their sources back
farther with them into the scarp.
The cap-rock

outliers they leave are often wooded.
Sight is of the senses

the one that most
lends itself to remove.
Each prospect for the looker-on is
his without trespass.

Across the tiers of houserows up from the river,

each profile shows what its volume
stretches to from its
mid-point out.
The ridges to their backs are in cloud
where the sheep pass

down from high summer grazing.
Their drove-road takes the turn of the hill.
Inviting the indicative,
the tie-bulwarked lawn above it has its

copy in the millpond's glaze.
Another figure appears who speaks English.
Upfield from the crude railing over a footbridge,

his alternately-forward

knees are caught
mid-stride.

ABOVE THE RED DEEP-WATER CLAYS

            Capacity is both how
much a thing holds and how
much it can do. From a solid
magnetized and very hot core, the earth

suffers itself to be turned outside.
Closest to its heart are the deepest submarine
trenches and sinks. Its lava finds

clefts there in the old uplifted crust,
the ocean floor a scramble. Wrapping at depth huge

shield volcanoes, the North Atlantic

down- and upwells, its denser layers making
room behind them through the blue-green shortest
wavelengths of light. Inside the cubic
yards it levies,
league by league, respiring, budgeting its heat,

it hides its
samenesses of composition through and through.

For the normal water level,
an ideal
solitary wave is surplus. Any wave's

speed is what it is
only if reversing it would render it still.
Surfaces are almost without feature
at Sea Disturbance number one.

When the wind stretches them, their wrinkling gives it
more to hold on to. Three is
multiplying whitecaps.
Spray blows in well-marked streaks at six.
In the foam-spewed rolling swell that takes a

higher number,

small and medium
ships may be lost to view for a long time.
Waves are additive. Doming

up on the tidal bulge into a storm's
barometric low,
the distances between them widen
as from the Iceland-Faeroes massif

leeward for another
three hundred miles southeast

they build unblocked. Little

enough for them
the first outlying gabbro
islets and stacks. These are not yet *The British
Countryside in Pictures*, not yet the shoals
off Arran in the Firth of Clyde.

That as all parts of it
agree in their low resistance to flow,

so should it be agreed to call it water.
To say of water that it floods both
forward and back through places
difficult to place demands that the ensouled

themselves make places for their parts of speech,
the predicates arrayed in
front of or behind the stated subject—

water, in the case at hand. Water

attains to its names because it shows as one thing
speech is about.
It shows as water.
To say no
more than that about however broad a sea is

plural already,
it says there must be something

else somewhere,
some second thing at least, or why say
how the thing shows? Before it can be taken

as a thing, as sea,
there have to have been readied for it other
possible-if-then-denied pronouncements—land,
the sky. Possible that
somewhere in the midst of waters there could

be such things as might be walked on,

hornblende and
felsite, quartzite, remnant
raised beach platforms, shales,
a cliff-foot scree.

Until given back accountably as
extant and encountered,
nothing counts. Nothing counts until
by reason it is brought to stand still.
Country. That it stands over

against one stands to reason. Not without
reason is it said of country that it
counters one's feet. To count as

groundwork for a claim about the ground,

reason must equate with country.
To be claimed as that, as country,
sand blown inland from the dunes must
equal its having landed grain by grain.

All grains have their whereabouts.
From emplacements in their clumps of

marram grass and sedges, some will be
aloft again and lime-rich
grain by grain will land.

Country is its mix of goings-on.
For these to tally, befores from
afters must at every turn divide.
Before it turns,
a cartwheel has its place to start from. It

stands there in place. In place an
axle's width away, another

parallel wheel is standing.
Not for long.
After each wheel in concert leaves its
first place for a second,

it leaves again at once a third and more. No more nor

fewer are its places on the strand than it has
time for in its turning.
Imprinted
one at a time,
these places are the lines the cart

makes longer at each landward place.
Not late for what goes

on there as its heft at each next place bears
down onto the loams and breaks them,
the seaweed-laden

cart is in time. Time is the cart's

enclosure. There for the taking, time is
around the cart,
which takes it from inside. Around
stones in the dry-stone dyke are

times out of mind,
those times the stones' embeddings let them go.
The hill-grazings
also are in time, and the three cows.
The blacklands are in time with their

ridged and dressed short rows of barley.
As it does around

bursts that for the places burst upon
abandon where they were before,
time holds around

the moving and the resting things.

FROM THE HOME PLACE

     Occurrences are
runnings-toward. From who knows what all
else time might have
sent there instead, a place is

run toward and reached and taken

up by a thing when a
thing takes place. What it
takes for a thing to happen is a place time lets it

pose or
be posed, arrested,
placed in a resting state
as clay and soured rushes are for
one first gabled end. Allotting things

constantly their whiles of
long or short standing, time is each stance's

circum-, its surround.
Circumstantial that the same one gabled end should
again take place as it had taken place one

instant before. As
wide as the first, as tall,
and though time brooks few repetitions,
a second gable

too time lets take place. Handedness

left and right affords in time a
front wall,

a back. Before on
top of it all time lets take place as well
a wheat-straw roof,
sod over coupled rafters must be laid
grass up.

Some of a house's sides are
biased, some upstanding. Because a

house has its sides,

so also does the air that meets them have its
clement and less clement sides.
To the sides a house is posed as are opposed as many
standing and inconstant

things as you please.
As distance is the room
away from an opposing, sided
instance or stance,
the out-of-doors

itself is sided by a house whose indoor ways makes
room outside. Going outside,
the out-of-doors is gone out

into.
From the standstill house out
in it
(and with room between) are

hayrick and byre, a road, the moss, discrete

potato-beds, their
grass-to-grass closed hinges.
Room is by the laws of growth at

play there outside for parts related
all as one in increase in the

one thing. Along a root
    Earthed over, earthed
        Over again,
    The rose end, heel end,
        Stolon, skin

outward through the loose mold
part by part take room.
Enlarged to *membrum*

virile now in size
and now to fist, they are

parts in relation. There are goods as

yield at the home place sometimes as at
other times
not. Time is
equable that way.
With no parts to it in itself, indifferent,

without relation, time offers
nothing to be carried back. Persons are
separate in time when they are living.
When certain maincrop tuberous parts go on being

missed at the hearth, back as

one again with time are persons now
outside it for good.
Against a bad

outside time,
relation

sometimes takes its sundry parts
inside.
To a first part entered in
relation with them there, inside,

the other parts are sometimes only
relatively other.
Seized as in every way
relative and to the first part's taste
are such late

outside parts as are now
stew and colcannon.

As back along the tongue
palatably are carried first one
bolus and more,

      The circle of the Same surrounds
          The circle of the stripped,
    Assimilable Other,
       Pharynx-housed, tipped
down through a tenser muscle to the gullet. Equal

each to what was wanted,
each timely part means that
apart from her
outside

are parts to be

made same, partaken, had as that one
thought is had in thinking present any
morsel she eats. Laid
hold of when she thinks
are parts that just before were

other for her,
anyone's,
apportioned out

between her and her fellows.
She thinks of everything that it is

passing in its little parts. When back at

once to those same parts are drift and
purport carried,
meaning grants the time to have
returned to her from not-yet habitable parts

just what it is she thinks of those parts as.
Until she has meant them
as that,

configurative parts are still futures,

they await being
thought about by her as having

each been fitted to its
suitable outward look.
All parts that show are in concord in their
standing over against her,

all are directed toward
what it is about them that she might mean.
As one who sees them, as one whose
self is drawn away to those
among them she sees,

no sooner is she
scattered there outside than she regains the more

that self immured in seeing them as such.

To meanings she takes part in with them, she
too belongs.
All parts that mean are
home to one still enough the same herself to be made
solute with them

inside what they mean.
Her domain
within them is the time they
take her to think.

Other for that time and
outside,
absolute,

are interrupting second parties.
High time that in his
proper person
one of them approach her now.
Others of her blood are there

around her,
inside. His having come could pass as a family call.

She can take it as that. So can he,

if beyond the frugal
greeting she tenders
she does not speak.

To address him
puts her at risk of what might follow
straightaway.
He would be sure to answer. It would be

colloquy then. Irrecoverably
past thereafter would this mute

present time be.
Among such parts as
give themselves to saying, each leaves a

now-no-more-than-recent part behind.
Another now arrives,
another. Nows
track that way, they multiply,
the gaps that let each new part differ from the last

they override.
At the same time it carries
on to its own undoing,
the present

keeps to itself. Resolute,

she presents the present
time and time again by keeping to hers.
Homesick for the Same, the One,
she gathers at the same time what she
watches for in him

and how it sits with her to see it. How
lavish of him that he is

there to see her. As long as she
thinks him that and goes on saying nothing,
she keeps everything at the
one same time. At the same time,

to think does not always

go without saying.
Articulations sometimes are come
out with,

they are aired,
my goodness, my

word what reach a party of the first part's
voice has for incarnate
third and second persons who can hear.
From its hollow up from
the open glottal cords,

the next column of

breath she issues still gives
nothing away.
Not so

The column after. As it leaves,
The lappets that she draws around it
Make it tremble so positions of the
Tongue, teeth, lips and jaw can sound it

abroad. Cast

forward from her thus are parts with their
own times each.

One does not have to turn to listen.
Airborne at the middle ear,
molecular,
each damped and stronger sound prompts its allied

hair-cell to fire. No more than a
smear at first,
the spell each sound is there for has its

onset and rise,
its temperings whose
play across the membranes no one
other repeats.
Dispersed toward him with the rest from what he

sees of her face,
the silences themselves are telling.
Of moment, every
nasal, glide and spirant,

every stop.
Time for them

all there is, these many, her express
fugitive and dative phonemes.
He has made them out.

Possibility. The possible.
It lets itself away when it divides.
Until from the sperm's
flagellates at its borders the ovum drinks

into it the decisive
sugar-tipped
one,

it does not sunder toward begetting.
Of whatever

later from the ovum might be led to the fore,

not a first move.
Not yet for it the cells in two
cell-making sets,
the paler, fleeter one set
given to engird the other. Inside it

instead,
divisible,

the ability of the still-
able-to-be-divided.
Such is the ovum's dower that until
cut for

it tends more and more

away from the same-centered.
Any actual
first upshot of its cleaving
is not to be fallen short of when it cleaves.
The nubile fecund. No more is she what she

might do in begetting
than that she might not ever do a thing.
Another body bids her to release

toward it through her own
all thwartings. The prospect
moves her. She calls it
back to her,

stilled. Attracted twice more,
she refuses.
Each next overtness that she thus puts by
wavers in her a little.
In tremolo

inside her for the time it lulls,
its span is from hidden

point to point only.
Keenest among the
new appeals are some so

partial to her that to

brave them strains her telling
outside from in.
Inside what has always been
one for her,
in what she would have be always

one and same still,
her singleness of heart maintains that
inward from the skin in hectored

adipose and neural reaches,
she is not herself.
The thing the self is singly wills away as
compound

the soma's

contrary points.
The digits, limbs, the trunk,

the head.
Division.
Hers are the striated muscles,
not hers

the smooth.
Neither the sometime blood nor
mucus is hers,

nor the congesting droplets
leaked by the adrenals

one by one inside.
The genes. Their cravings for the unconceived.
She would make fast
against these anew
the word that they are peril. Desiring,

winsome and desired,

ahead of herself
already is she to the times at hand of

issue that will be her double.
The capable are those who through their
fine intervenings bring her

back into phase.

Herself among them,
they would have her put on continence wherever she
fares in her rounds. Made willful
bid to by them in her is that,
uncleaved,

the ovum contains
along with the companionable
yea to division
the nay. Dominion over

both poles is at issue.
The will wills
doing a thing. Determining it

action-worthy,
it wills it done.

Only for as long as that thing is
not done does the will
have it to will. With such
thrust has it willed it often that unless it now
nills it as well

it risks
losing it to the act.
Lost to it then would be a thing without which
the will cannot do. The force to

do a thing will not have best it any

loss of that force.
To maintain it as its ownmost thing, it holds

apart for the thing, inside,
the poles
between which it moves.
When the willed thing traffics to be acted

out of and leave,

so fastened to it are they that they stretch
almost outside. The wider the cleft
between them,
the more the will has to do. Let the
yes to division entertain inside whatever

increase it will. The cleft will still be
internal only for the no that
keeps held pressing inward through

piety
and by lay custom and rule
that force each ovum has to be either
cleaved or not cleaved.

With the mother wit
not to be cleaved,
potential
stays for itself its chances
never to be determined from outside.

Each begotten thing is

determinate only.
Embodied,
it has to start somewhere. It has to

leave off somewhere else.
Those are the terms.

Instead of staying
capable,
an ovum might have had the cleft enacted on it
once and for all.
Upon forgotten

forebears long ago,
it rested to send on rememberers.
Of one's dead precursors,

the progenitrix first.
Emergent,
second,
at the ready,

the progenitor,
outside.

Out of their physical

ways together,
coupling,
out of the two,
the many in the strain that will have issued

through them into
one's own time.
One is franchised to suppose

one's own line back toward them as a sum of instants

willed and unwilled. Among those
unwilled was the first,

a streak
so faint within the blastula that it might be time
alone that divides.
Thrown to it soon had been
its promised groove with ridges. Soon

the ridges were plates, the plates
a tube.
Impertinent, the thorough

talking-to that one's conditions gave one
right from the start.

There was a time when they had not yet had their

say with one. Since one had
not yet started, the whole of what
might have been was
not yet broken into. Not meted
out for one yet were the provisos if and

how it would be.
One still might not in time be given
over to a body,
it was all still able to go

any way at all.

Against the rudiments that tell one what came first,
longing

wills from the long ago the very longest,
it wills that one
impossibly had given some first

terms to oneself.
Not all. Not
whom one had come from in the strain
on one's only

chance to.
Not when.
Incontestable that in the
timing of it
once and for all

there had to have been at
all times
the accomplished,

the already-come-to-pass.
From the appropriateness of any one of them either

happening or not,
there had to have slipped in
once and for all by turns
the many things.
The course toward one had been

set upon. Under

way already was the next least change.
Leading on,
another and still others followed.
It is when one wills such former changes

stopped somewhere in their train that is
itself the beginning.

Until given out later as what has been
risen from,

origin has not happened.
It cannot be returned to, having
never yet been.
Able to be longed for

rearward through forgottenness are

kin willed whole.
These are the originals,
the participant

young among one's people who had
not yet bred.
Inseparable in them from what could
not have been that was
is what was not that

could have been.
Remembered as
phantasms only,
their bodies' members are

assigned them anew.
There had been

drugget to wear, and worsteds,

flax.
Their fathers were tenant farmers.
The ground they lived from was
not theirs by law.
Its statute acres in the straths and leas were

wanted for grass. Subject to
rack-rent, tithes and cesses,
in arrears,

they were sent away so as to be

shut of.
They were the expelled.
Modesty would have had them give up being seen
anywhere at all.
Not in keeping with the prevalent due

measure was it of them
to outlast on other
poorer ground
the riddances ordained.

The bogs were left them.
Leached and stony
hillsides were left,

the moors and marches. Up from bare
rock on the islands out of layered

kelp-bed cuttings and sand
they built
soil for their husbanded seed-tubers,
all roots the axes for new
second-order shoots,

new third-.

Around the sink each
bud is in its loading of starches,
there is by enough

more there for it than it needs
that the canopy

too can grow. The tuber draws down
into it through its stalks its assimilate carbons.
When shading at last starves it inside,
such are its

root dry matter stores that any refuse
keeps it from frost.
Replicate,
the bulbs were of their element
if just as patently

not it.

The sheer spread of them in their sets
repeated them as items.
They were sown wherever.
Taking up more and

more again nearby
an earth that in itself
could not be eaten,

they gave
bone and sinew cheap.

Potatoes were the one food. So

peopled did they let it be
that heritable plots kept being halved.
Marriage was to the ground.
The young were often not

seen by one another until
joined in their match.
So they could live with someone they chose,

daughters engineered their own abductions.
Landless sons were either

buried so or they left.
Among the still unwed there were no longer
strips to share out.
Land promised that when
dug for across a straggle of

waste and upland holdings,
its bulbs could be fit wards
for some few only

only for a time.
Digging was in the fall.
With the stock of them
low by late summer,

the aftermost were taken

raw nearly.
This slowed their transfer through the body.
It let them last.
The new ones were still of too little bulk.
They were looked toward with the more

care this time. Covered
one by one, each plant had

fastened to it by airborne
spores at their tips
a down of long threadlike fibers.
These would not whisk away.

It was all
one for the plants
that the infestation was theirs.
Their leaves turned black. They withered.
When loosed by

hand at last from under their
inches of soil lid,
the potatoes were black too. Their skins

scraped at
made the tissue inside

collapse to a pulp.

There was no drying them out that they might be food.
Some foraged
inland for a while on

cresses, herbs, wild cabbage,
silverweed,
young furze.
Put off their plots by bailiffs,

some cornered
cattle where they could and bled them.

Plover and

grouse were caught,
as on the grounds of the estates,
in thickets,
bramble-covered
mantraps caught the ones who poached.

Itinerants at the shores took sand-eel,
periwinkle, dulse and limpet.
Ropes lowered them to the cliffs for
seabirds' eggs. They tramped for fluke.

There were no

songs for these labors.
Songs in the field are for acts that hearten,
acts that daily

lend the songs cause.
Depleting daily what fed them,
they were not tilling, not reaping.
With nothing to
grow it in,

there was nothing to grow.
Called back again was a hunger complied with

often before.

To be mindful that
stuffs had been inside one in less
straitened times was at
least not nothing. It could not

serve as enough.
Wherewithal was what was wanted.
Until against its
lining from inside there could again be
shove there,

the stomach would have curvature in
recall alone.

The want it shrank to at its least full
left it pleated and flat. Withdrawn to a
cylinder now, each had belong to it

its having to do its wanting.
Hunger was the state it compressed to.
Nothing differed for it from its
having to do without.

Cholera came with eating the black potatoes.
Out from their

sod and wattle huts

the mendicant were at large,
some having pawned their clothes.
Those who were fevered brought

typhus with them in the
lice on their skin. These they passed
on to their private donors.
Public
outdoor relief was gruel in iron cauldrons

five feet high. Undercooked,

its Indian meal pierced the intestine.
Urban soup-kitchens
stored their food in safes.
A hundred could be fed at one

six-minute sitting,
their dole poured into white-enameled
quart-size basins with
spoons attached to chains.
The few admitted to the overrun workhouses slept

four to a straw pallet in stalls
divided by sex. Outside,
there was no want of

rocks to break.
The men were to level the ground for roads.

Onto their shovels,
they scooped their noon allotment of meal and then
wet it.
The gang's weakest were kept day-long
watch over by the many

waiting to take their places when they fell.
It was one's chance. One wanted to stay
far enough from them not to be
seen keeping watch.

To persist.
To continue to be. It would take

more from the hunger urging it than
adroitness and mettle. It could take
more than one had. One needed

others to withdraw if one were

oneself to go on living.
Some of one's fellow
watchers withdrew.
They crossed to Liverpool. There was
America and the ships.

Death was a thing to leave for, as were other
workhouses still.
The one who stayed there

lived from such leavings.
Waiting out the rest of them,

he watched.
The gang's work went along. Overtaxed,
they were a blend now of the able and the not.
There was no

hiding from the watcher in those not able
the stare their
eyes put on. He had seen this

change in them,
had caught them being past what it would
take them to stay.
Of the five likeliest,
welcome would be coming to him soon from

the one dispatched first.
That was the one who would host him,
the one he would kill.
Not to know which

spared him little. He would be one

among them soon at their fellow's ruin.
How that would sit with them was

not to be weighed.
He was no less the self-accused
for being kept there
near them by need.

They had faltered the more.
Near enough to be
spoken to,

they were on their
feet, still, as

he was on his.

Across the intervals from
his side to each,
it was no one else's to speak
aloud to them in their hearing
his entreaty that

one of them fall.
He spoke it to himself instead with

no favor.
What the self came back to always
was what it owed.
In the languor of his waiting to eat,

patience was his having it go

on for him as he watched that there would be for
him too with any
thrust of it
the brute
resistances each time against the shovel,

the lift and heave.
Roads headed off to no clear purpose and were
added to.

So were the walls.
The evicted dying sought out
cover along them.
Whatever their attire,

their faces pressed
naked into an air consenting that they rend it

each cheekbone and brow.

What they had thus far abided,
they wanted not to show.
Corps of them in the one bloodline

huddled together in the ditches,
under gaps in a hedge.
Not all could hide. The land was laid
impress on across it in the light of day
by those it at the last

against all striving secured to its skin.

Its pace in taking them was not the same from
one to the next.

The hardier were entwined for
weeks sometimes
in the limbs of their expired kin. When they
themselves were released,
the lot could then be hauled away to any

quicklime pit at hand
or to a mound of the uncoffined.
Between the files of keening mourners,

it was often not far.
Those stretches widened.
The land was taking
back to itself in its being

the people it had let conceal it.
Belonging to it
forever now with the virgin dead were
those who had paired.
On such land that would not let them be,

errant of them to have
come together and made more.
First and second,
lover and beloved,

it had emerged for them to know better than
almost all
that third thing wanting

lives from,

separation,
a space to reach through to the one desired.

Where it had started was in oneself.
Another who had not
been there before had passed through
out of her own

toward and into one's body.
Imbuing it, making it want,
she had loosed in it as lack thereafter

a room
she only could fill.
Flush with the room inside were intervals
outside that
kept him from her. These he could

close through so that
she could be touched.

What let her front him

just where the nerve-sheaths end were those last
differences between what
was and was not her body. All

verge over there,
her fascia in the mesh behind it flooding,
she was able to have
shake within her until it gave way what had been

too much herself.
While for his
blandishments with her
he needed the room
air makes,

time itself had been making more and more

room between lovers.
Not possible for long one's

sexual wanting
when one not eating keeps
wanting to eat.
There were sin's wages.
Discord was succession and event. As lovers'

ardour withdrew and they were not
apt any more at sequel,
what they passed
on there now accorded with the whole.

For Whitehall,
Parliament and money,

desire was now the realm of the elect and

they were not home.
The gatelodge was still empty. Avenues of
yew and fir past parkland

held to the domed rotunda for their lines.
At both ends of the prodigal broad central front,

entablature,
plump Coade-stone cherubs at their
easels and harps.
Sculpted into its own plantations,

the absentee's demesne was with the grassy rough

tracts outside it not
two things
but one.

From the ground up
anywhere outside or in,
a folk impossibilized had cleared between them all
the null
allowances that let each part be seen.

Impunity for each was from the first its separable
contour and mass.
Chance had so worked them that in
company now with fossils of the open-field strips

were low sod fences that eclipsed them.
Care did not break

up any more the staid
concord there was between the things in view that were
not one's to eat.
They were affairs of the eyes for grazing
sheep and cattle only.

Secreted

outside them,
if across the Irish Sea,
were figures with another less fell life. Theirs

alone was its prospect,
this Garden With No One In It left to

err and be killed.

BACK

A place can be disposed so
ill toward them that many
lives are untimely.
To a nation by one's
birth to it belongs the law to carry

through to their ruin
all untimely lives.

Securing to it through their mothers' travail
all bodies that can make do,
capacity stays
ahead of what happens,

it fits it

out for them first that they might
feed and pass waste.
A first thing the neonate

mouth had been for in hunger was to seize.
Emerged from,

its capacity to
be what it was had not yet
fallen away to the later
moves it would make to
fix it,

the mouth did
not yet have words.
There were the folds of

lips around it and
cheeks,
the baby hull from the throat down
walled in its scarfskin film,

the cells

flattened now without their water.
The brain itself the skin was of a
piece with already.
Soon enough,
it would have to be for more,

would have to consign
inside,
as through the tissue behind it,

each lambent trace.
Only this first once had that perhaps not been a

must yet.

A person
starts out and lives. One moment
on from that start—
still breathing and imperfected,

still in the way—
the body has regards that

tell upon it.

A person goes on being led to find as
looked-for
the things in his ken. There are
items there.
These guard against his being

nowhere at all.
If being was at first not
yet for the body
the entities that had

made their ways there,
not yet was the light of day
a showing only.

Though finite
beings were there with the needful
spacing between,
the light they showed in also hid
their infinite remove from how they might

never in fact have showed.
The spacing

itself showed.
Of the newborn only one
moment before,

it was all that had showed.

The allotted
spacing,
the room,
the nothing-there: so

stretched had it been
eventually
that it was

his to break through.
Just given

outlet to,

he was perhaps still
of the nothing-there at
advent for that
first blink only,

nothing
alone it may have been
that skin was pulled
back to at first.
There was a nothing of his

own now.
It was accommodating,

this room his inner
parts took for
what they might do.

For a body's holding-parts to be
arrived at and hold,
their spacing must from the first be drawn out as much
forward as
back.

From then on more and

more it is to their one last turn
that by their drivenness
they fill and empty.
The cerebellum will in time

expand. There as its
bent already in the size alone
will be its drive

away from the short-lived body.
Much that is
not drive
ranges there
outside. Into it

forward from the body's organs as
against the outside will be

prostheses,
place-holdings
added to the body's destined place.
Some are there early.

Tall,

heavy, charged and
white on the low horizon,
a block print of clouds
breasting the rain-cleared air will be at
hand for the child in

Mother Goose.
While there will have been
sons in both theaters who had
not come home,

ready as well will be
the slots and tabs of wooden

jig-saw pieces for

"An English Cottage Garden,"
the border intact by the first
Christmas after

WW II.
Inside a backyard
tent at night,
not knowing where the

sky stops will be enough the same as

knowing he will die.
Executive,

one's being
implements its own completion.
One's call from the start

is from ahead where there is nothing.
The body in
advance thus always of what a person
in itself
is,

it shows along the way as having not yet

done what it must. To have
done with it at last means
no relation, not

air anymore,
not heat, no tonic
likelihood nor interval,
no remnant,

nothing to see.
Being is what there is
when beings that had come to light are
no longer there.
Being quenches itself on its

out-of-this-world pull forward.
Against the end itself if also

from it,
craven,
false,

the imagined turnaround

backward in time.
He could
retrace in reverse each
percept, act and wish that had
made up his life,

each one could be discarded, he could
think it away.

When one tends back,
it can be thought to have happened
first for a little
that the body held becalmed from before it was born

the give-and-take

fondling of its begetters,
that ruffle they had left it in its
being made.
To caress means to go
on to what end,

what reason
ever would there be to stop
when still on call
beyond the place one reaches toward

lie other skin and
progeny,

how many in the line descending would it
ever be enough to
quit with just there?

Becalmed outside on the nascent
body perhaps
once only was a
first light graze.
With the nerves inside perhaps at

rest still if
poised,

it had become as well in less than
no time at all
the last
least trifling

ever to be let pass.
Skin had not yet had to have a
back to it.

Paper-thin,

it had happened to have been brushed.
Outside the mother's
aperture now,
so much for the dark.

Since Beginning
itself begins the one death one is
born toward
and will not bear,
the light was

again at once

closed over. Closed over at
once in the opening was every

other look
the skin might have had.
When cleared of that first

flutter across it was the newly
brought-to-light skin,
the shift to its
second light had been
too quick to see.

In the run at once
into it and then

on,

the first could not now be gone
back to.
Back would from then on have to be

a light made fast.
Sizings of
egg white had been spread on single sheets with
citric acid,

salt and silver nitrate.
Cameras for a century

had held the gel inside in

just the right place.
1946. From halide
grays that had taken
eight years before,

fine black and white points neighbor
end to end across
each of the several hundred,

The British Countryside in Pictures,
a book of photographs in green
flexible boards.
So little too
early for him are these likenesses that it will be

months only
before he is born to die.
Tucked around that moment back into his
absence in the pictures,

he is reconceived.

His body having not yet
differed from it,

any one scene's plenty is his
death-mask inverted.
Reversible to the eye
the path above the foreground yarrow and gate,
a plough-team in the middle distance.

The span by span erasure of him
spectral there
inside the picture's

outside-of-time
safe spatial harbor,

he is in repeal,
exempt,
the coppice to the left behind the rise
a boyhood haunt.